Unbelievable Pictures and Facts About Great Danes

By: Olivia Greenwood

Introduction

The Great Danes breed of dog is becoming increasingly popular. They make excellent pets and they are rather large in size. They have fun personalities and are known to be quite clumsy and klutzy. Learn more about these wonderful dogs right here today.

Are Great Dane dogs popular in America?

The answer is a big yes. Great Danes are very popular dogs in America. They are highly ranked in terms of their level of popularity.

How do people describe Great Danes?

There are many words which people use to describe the Great Dane dog breed. They have been described as "clumsy" and "great with children".

What age do Great Danes live up until?

The sad news is that Great Danes do not live for very long. In comparison to other dog breeds, they live very short lives. Their life expectancy is around 8-10 years of age.

When did Great Danes become an official breed?

The great Dane breed became officially recognized in 1887, although it has been a breed for much longer.

Has a world record ever been won by a Great Dane?

Zeus was the name of a Great Dane who won the Guinness World Records. He won the record for being the tallest dog in the entire world. When he stood on his hind legs he was extremely tall. No dog was taller than Zeus.

Do Great Danes grow quickly?

Great Danes are known throughout the world for growing really fast. From the day they are born till 18 months of age, they keep growing at a rapid pace.

Are there any common illnesses associated with this breed?

Owners of Great Danes are encouraged to feed their dogs smaller meals instead of bigger meals. The truth is that these dogs are prone to bad bloating. Their stomachs can become twisted and it can become very dangerous. The way to avoid this happening it not to feed them one big meal but rather a few smaller meals which are broken up over a specific period of time.

Have Great Danes been used in the military?

Many years ago there was a beautiful Great Dane with the name of Nuisance. Nuisance was enlisted officially in the Navy. This meant he was allowed to travel with the Navy men on trains for free. He was a very smart and wonderful dog.

Is there a nickname used for the Great Dane dogs?

The nickname often given to great Danes are "the Apollo of the dog world".

How long has the Great Dane breed been around for?

There is no exact time period that can be established for how long these dogs have been around for. Although Great Danes were seen in ancient Egypt.

Have Great Danes been famous in anything?

Once again the answer is a big yes. Great Danes have been very popular in many things including cartoons. Great Danes have featured in popular shows such as Marmaduke, The Jetsons, and Scooby Doo.

Have any governors favored these dogs?

The answer is yes. The governor named William Penn who was the governor of Pennsylvania loved great dane breeds. He was known to everyone for his love of great danes.

Are Great Danes official dogs of any places?

It is interesting to learn that these dogs are official dogs of not one but two places. They were the national dog of Germany in the year of 1876. In addition in 1967 in Pennsylvania, they were the state dog.

What colors do these dogs come in?

These dogs come in all sorts of colors. There are actually six distinct colors which they come in. They are also known to have 3 distinct types of markings. The colors are mantle, fawn, brindle, blue, black and harlequin.

Does the Great Dane require a vast amount of exercise?

You may be surprised to learn, that although these dogs are rather large in size, they do not actually need that much exercise. This makes the perfect pet. They do need a big garden to run around and play in, this makes them very happy.

What type of size are these dogs?

Great Danes are known for being a particularly big dog breed. In fact, many people joke and refer to them as "horses". In terms of height, they are around 30 inches tall more or less. In terms of weight, they weigh around 175 pounds give or take.

What was the reason behind the breeding of these dogs?

The real reason why Great Danes were bred was for hunting reasons. However, they also were used to as guard dogs.

Where did these dogs obtain their name?

Way back in the 19th-century people tried to change the name of these dogs. However, the name eventually led to Great Dane and this is the name they have been called ever since.

Which dog breeds do Great Danes originate from?

The great Dane dogs are made of three different dog breeds. They are made up of the mastiff dog, the Irish wolfhound dog, and greyhound dogs.

Exactly where do Great Danes originate from?

Believe it or not, great Danes have absolutely no Danish origins. The name may suggest that they have Danish roots. However, this is not the case, the Great Dane dog breed actually originates from Germany.

Made in the USA
Coppell, TX
14 June 2020

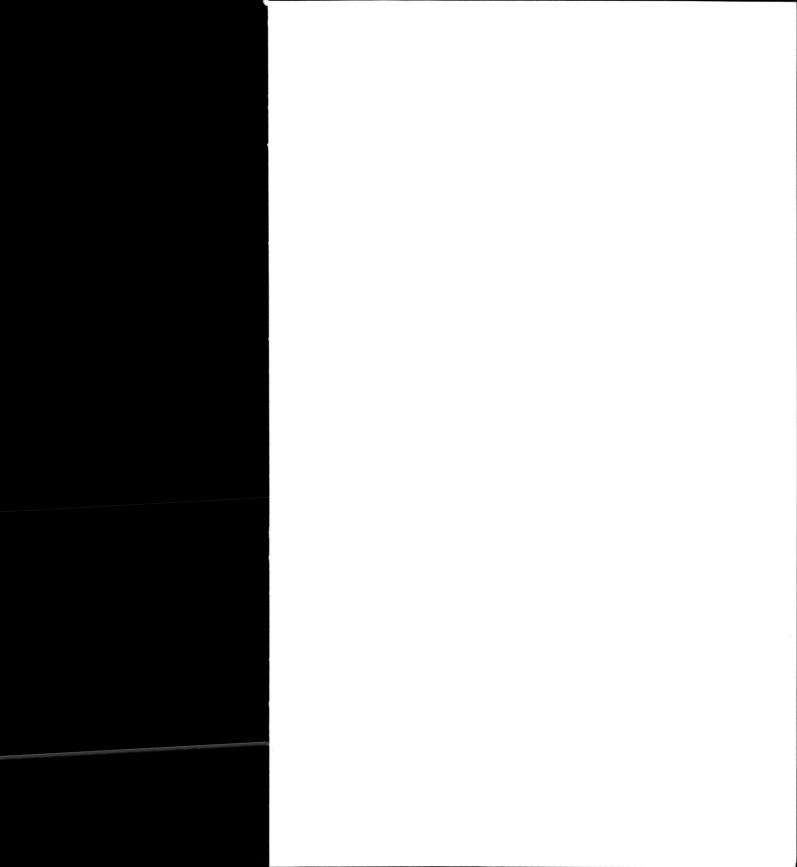

ISBN 9781079903836

9 781079 903836

Goodness Falls

a novel by ty roth